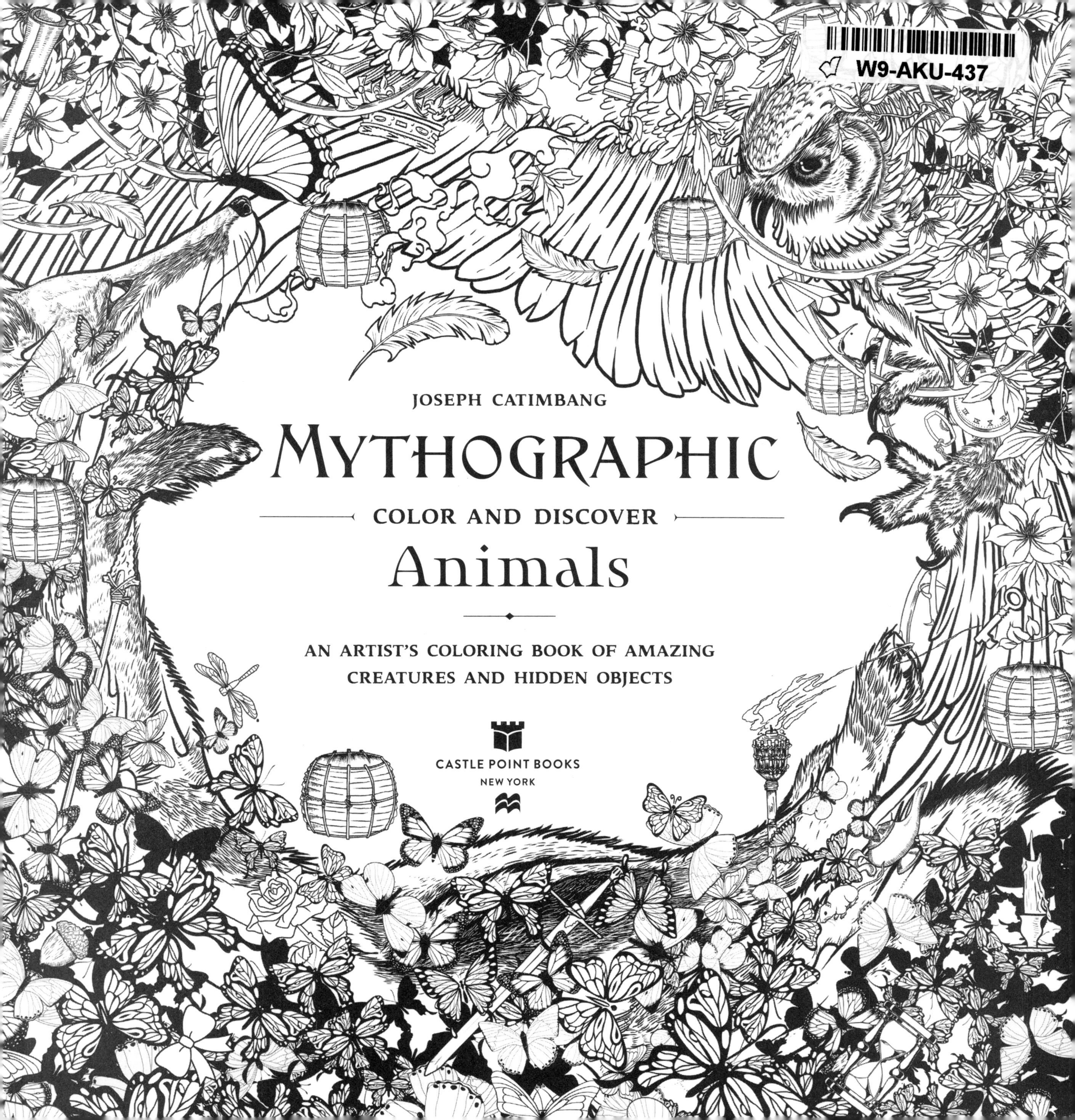

JOSEPH CATIMBANG

MYTHOGRAPHIC

COLOR AND DISCOVER

Animals

AN ARTIST'S COLORING BOOK OF AMAZING CREATURES AND HIDDEN OBJECTS

CASTLE POINT BOOKS
NEW YORK

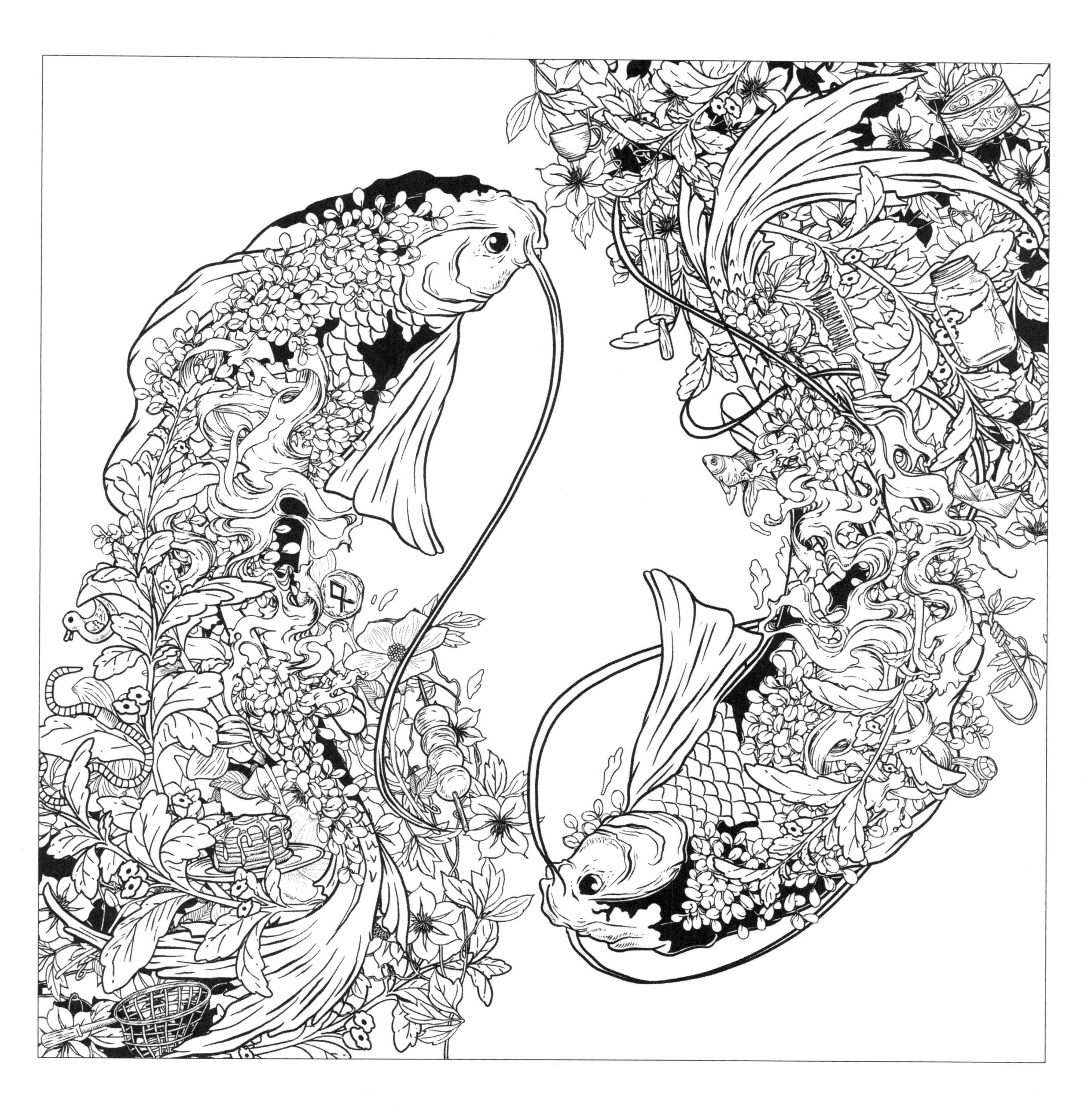

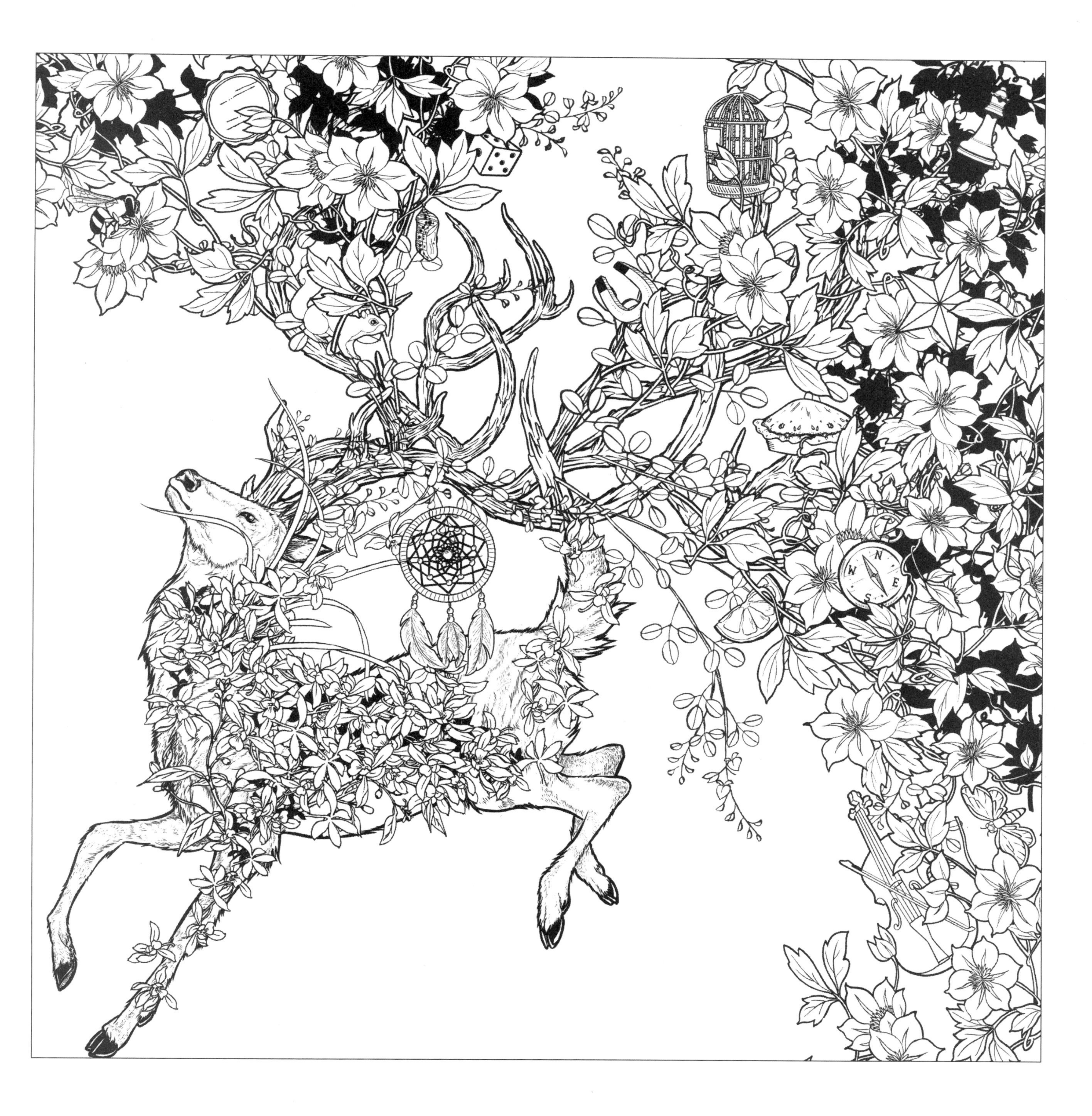

INK
INK

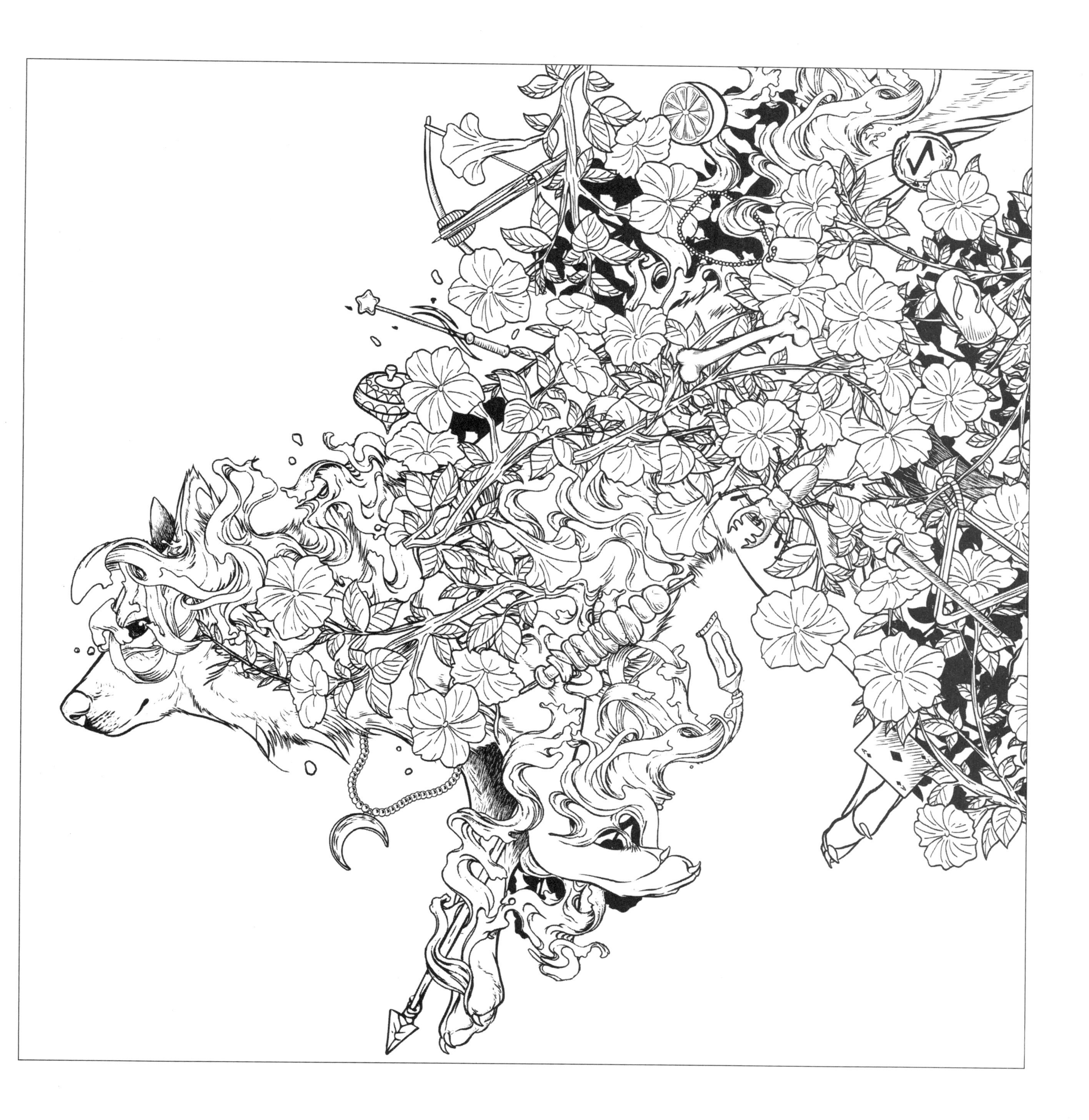

SOAP

TICKET

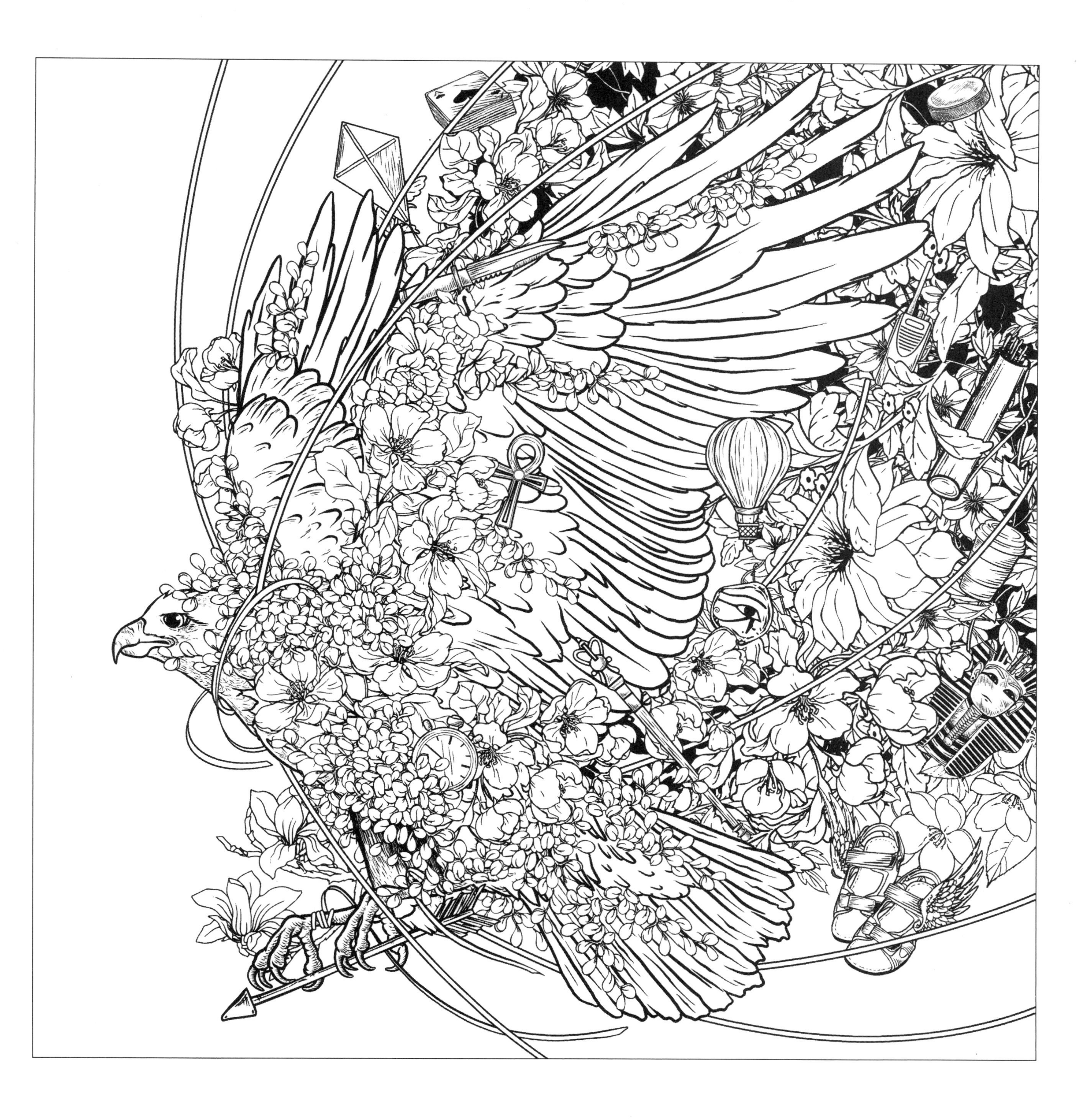

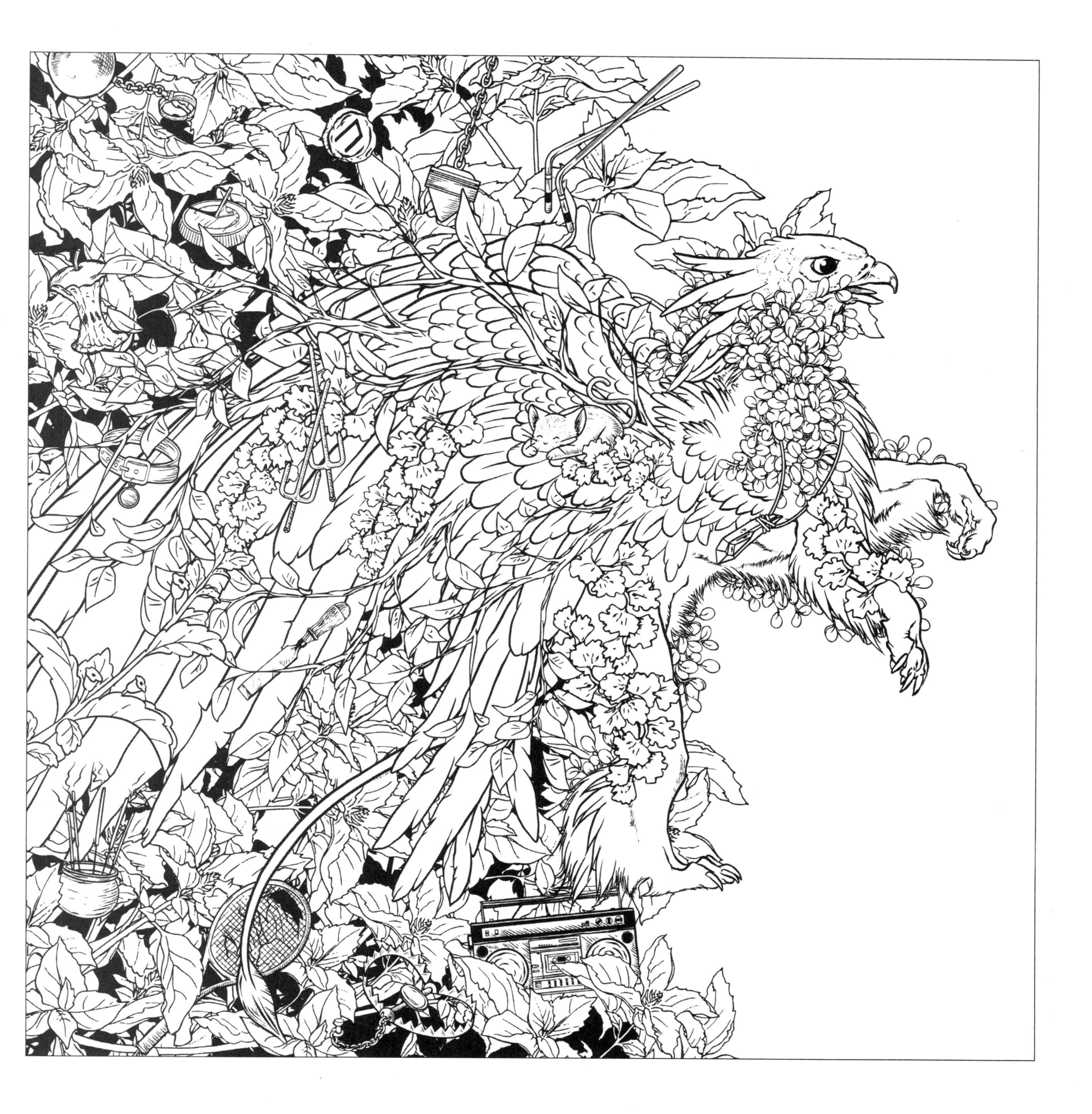

CHIPS

25

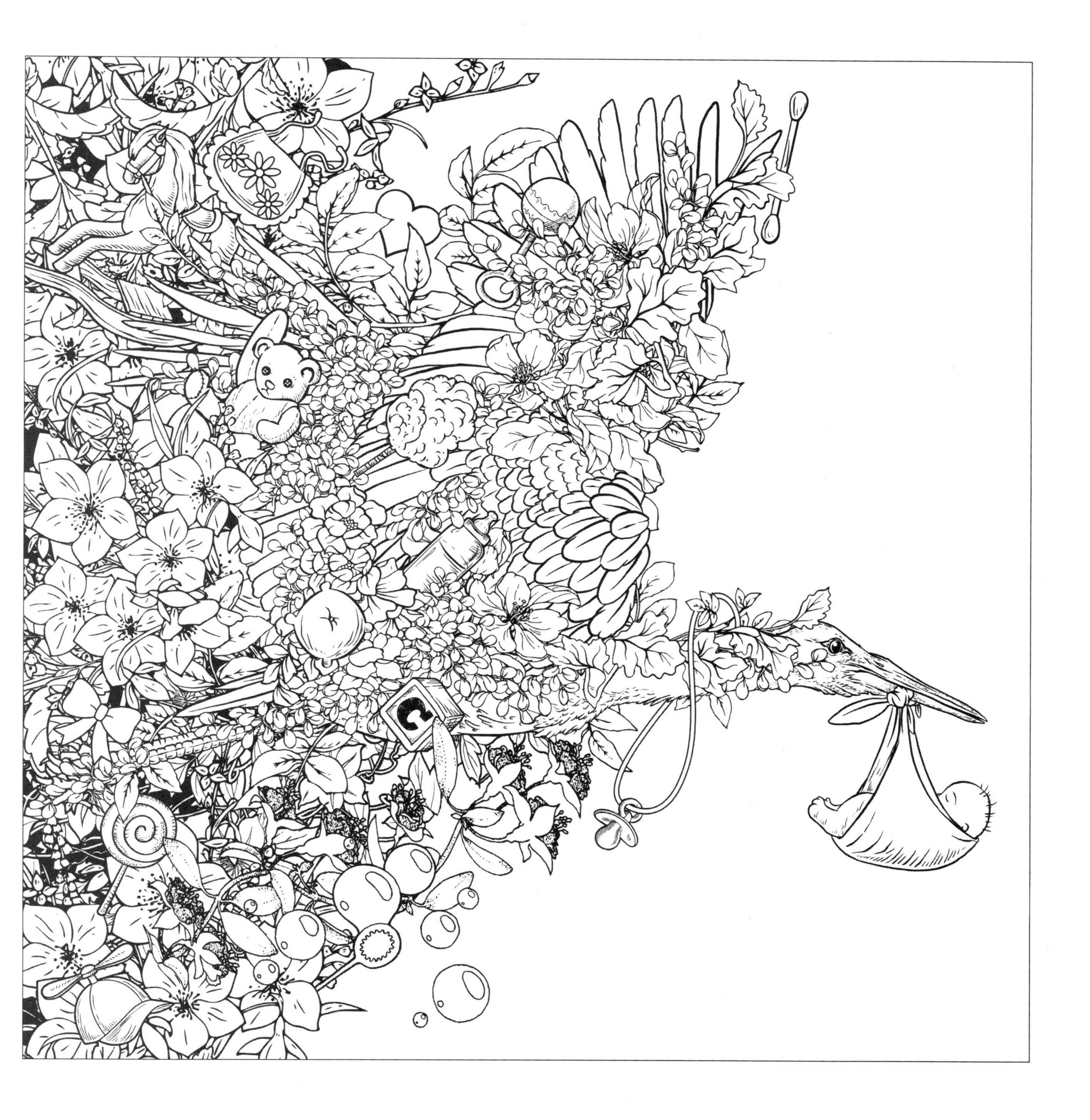

BINGO

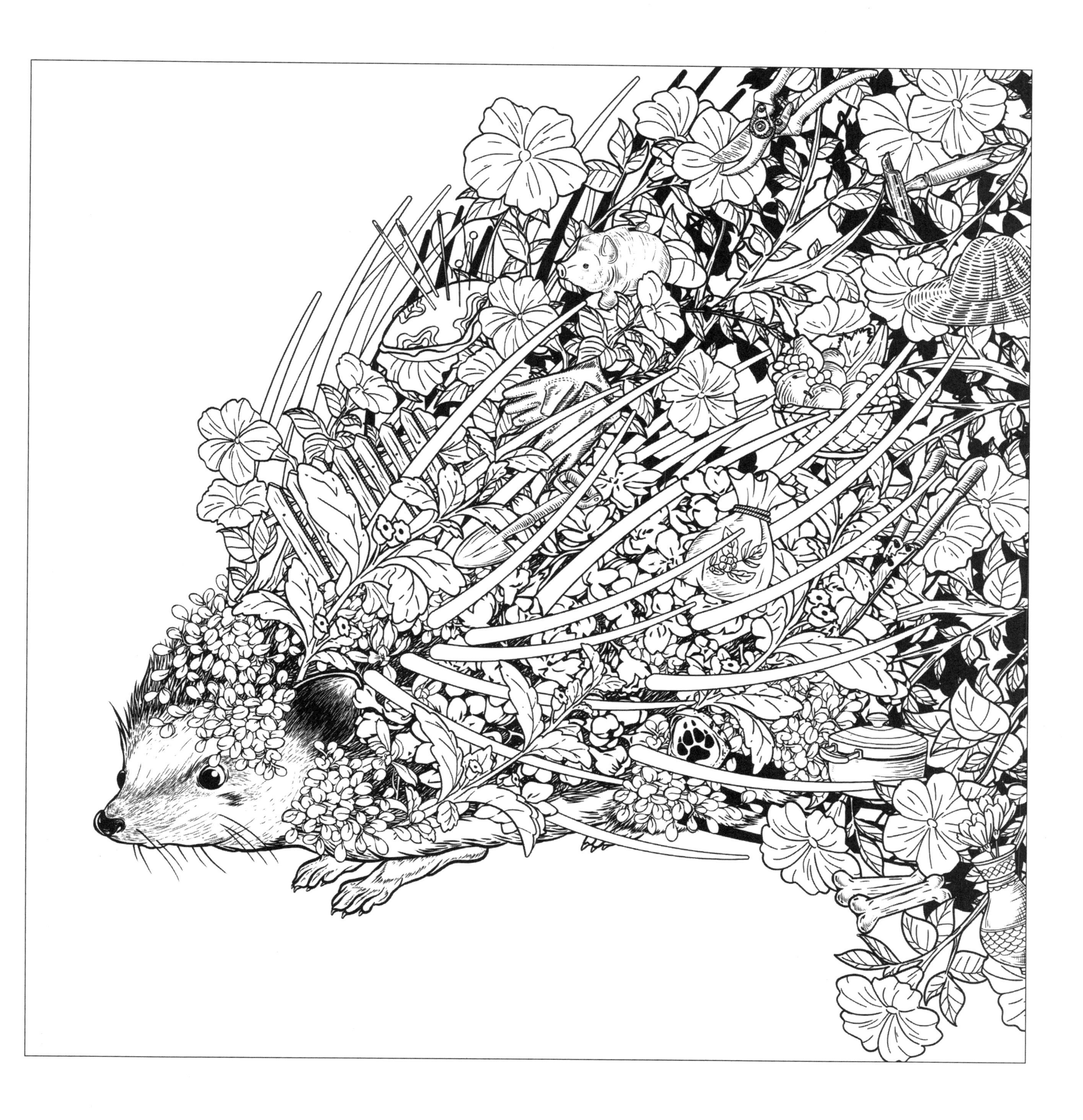

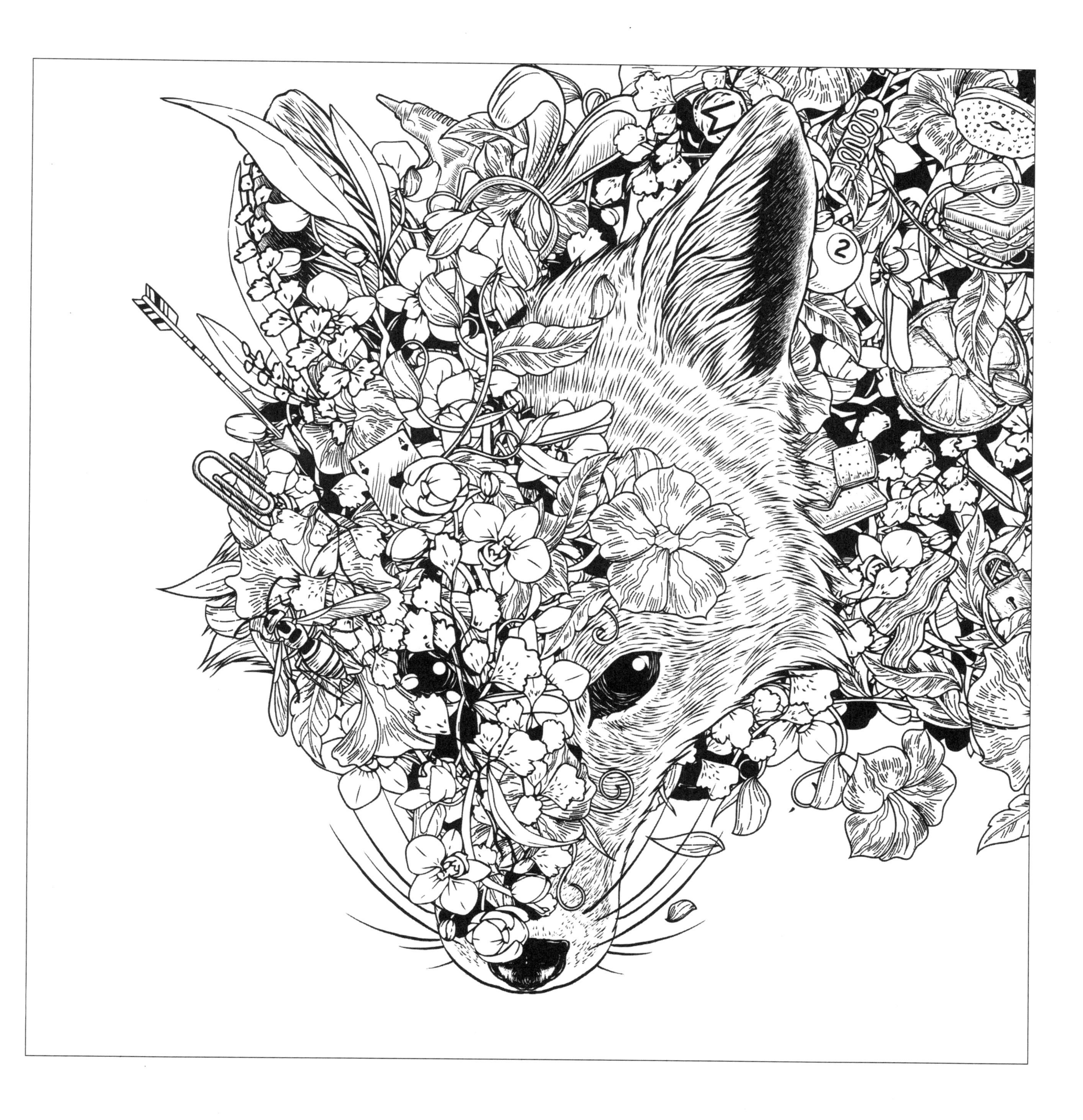

121816

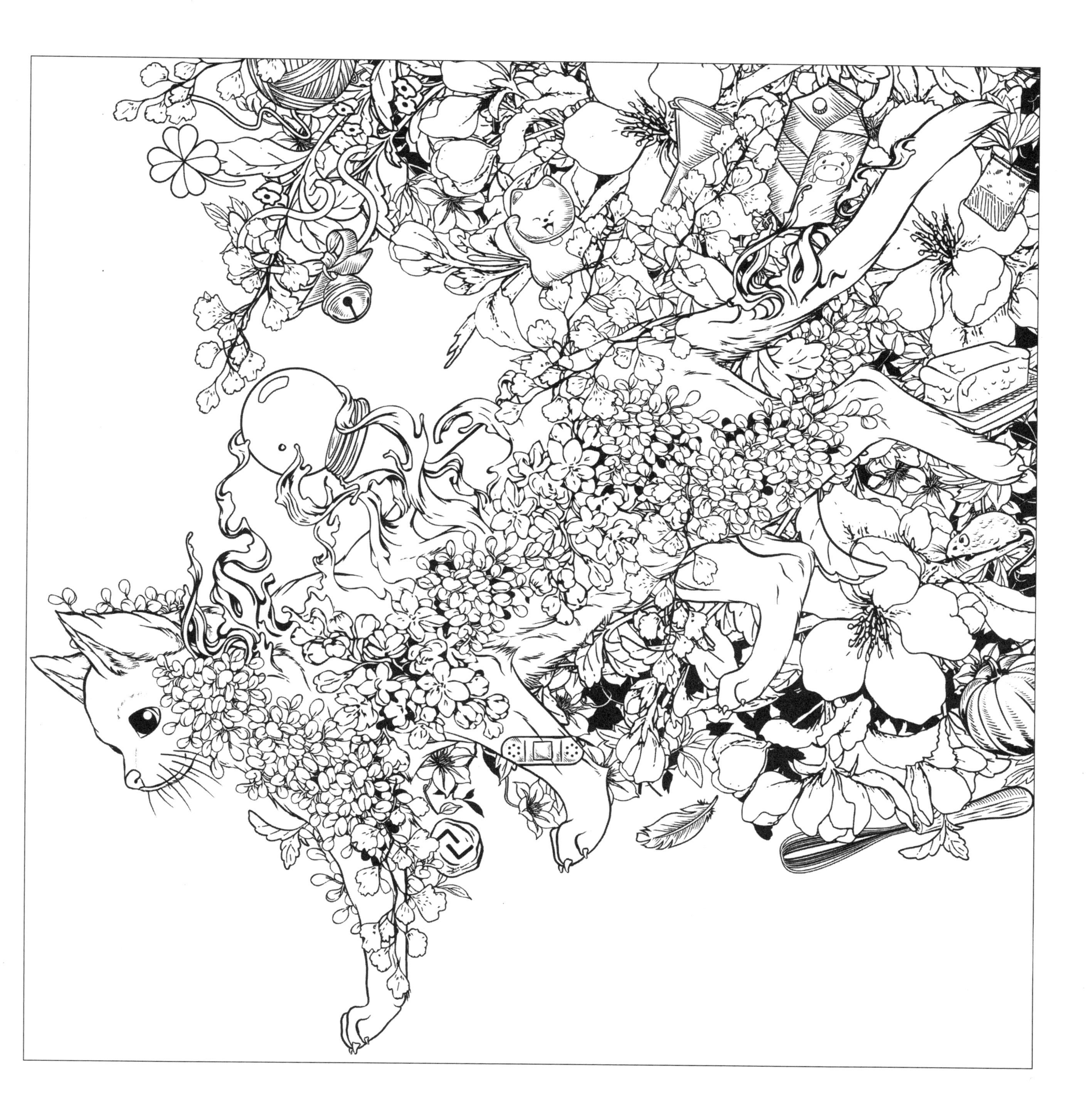

3

092515
ON
CE

2
100

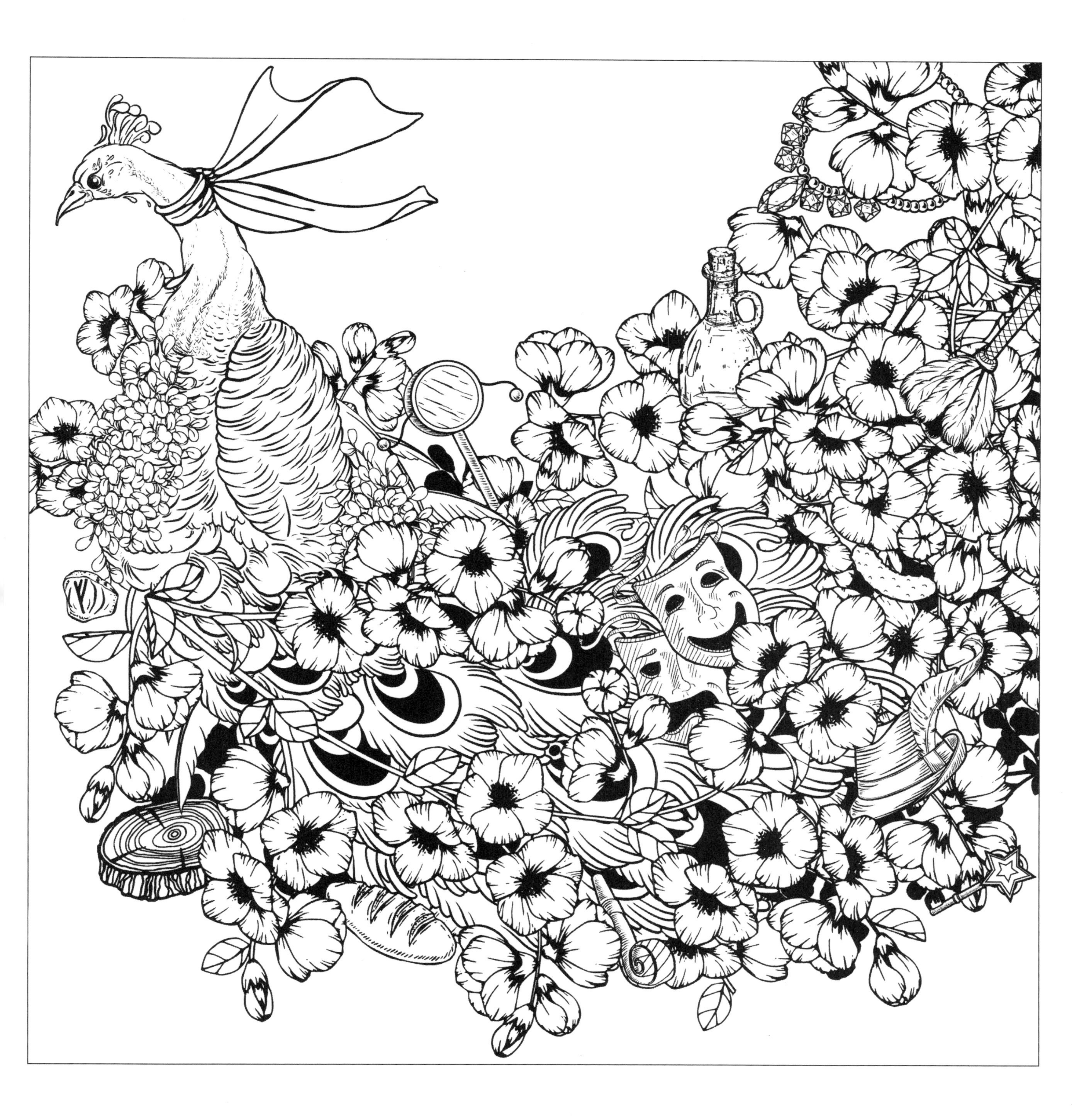

1
B

HIDDEN OBJECTS REVEALED

COVER

1 Sword 2 Snail 3 Book and Pencil 4 Pocket Watch 5 Hummingbird 6 Mask 7 Mouse 8 Dragonfly 9 Hourglass 10 Chess Piece - King 11 Acorn 12 Spear 13 Ribbon 14 Crown 15 Key 16 Rose 17 Lamp 18 Scroll 19 Paper Airplane 20 Candle

KOI

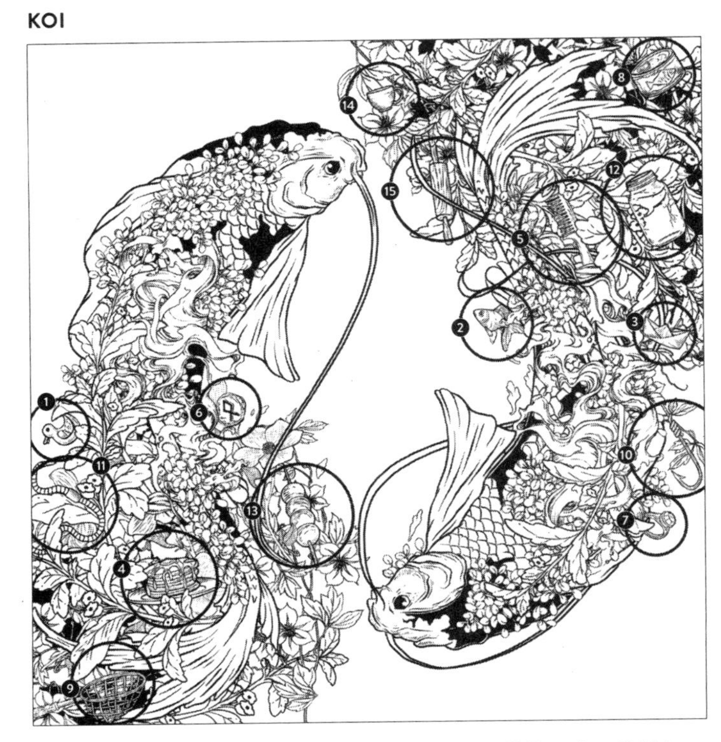

1 Rubber Duck 2 Goldfish 3 Origami - Paper Boat 4 Pancakes 5 Hair Comb 6 Rune Stone 7 Ring 8 Canned Sardines 9 Fishing Net 10 Fishhook 11 Worm 12 Glass Jar 13 Fishball 14 Teacup 15 Rolling Pin

RHINOCEROS

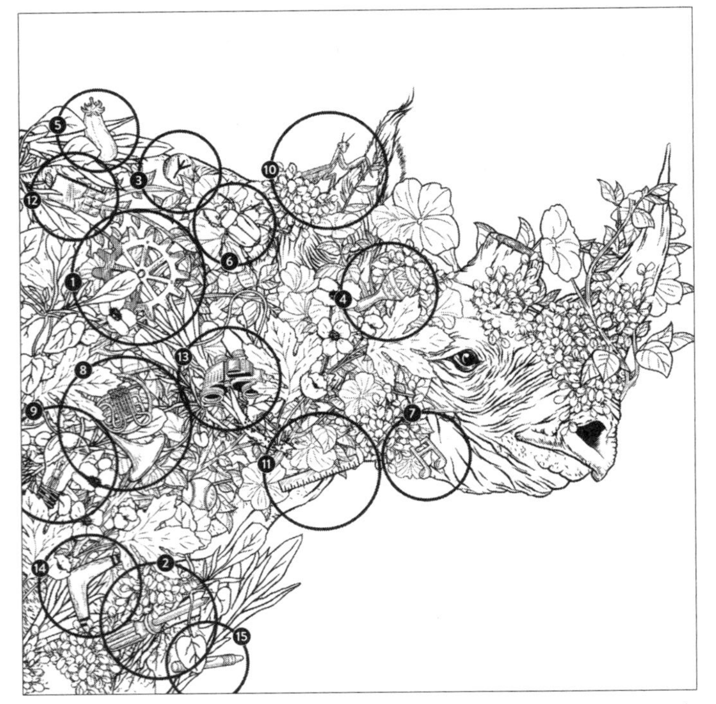

1 Gear 2 Screwdriver 3 Rune Stone 4 Maraca 5 Eggplant 6 Scarab 7 Music Note 8 French Horn 9 Light Bulb 10 Praying Mantis 11 Ruler 12 Chocolate Bar 13 Binoculars 14 Boomerang 15 Crayon

UNICORN

1 Chess Piece - Knight 2 Mace 3 Carrot 4 Harp 5 Helmet 6 Axe 7 Star Pendant 8 Chameleon 9 Umbrella 10 Flute 11 Ladybug 12 Fork 13 Lock 14 Scissors 15 Candy 16 Glasses 17 Diamond 18 Paint Brush

STAG TREE SPIRIT

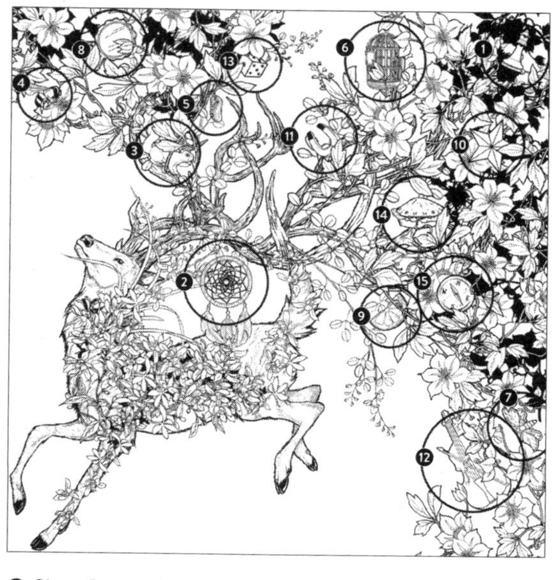

❶ Chess Piece - Queen ❷ Dreamcatcher ❸ Squirrel ❹ Bee ❺ Cocoon ❻ Birdcage ❼ Moth ❽ Hand Mirror ❾ Slice of Lemon ❿ Star ⓫ Magnet ⓬ Violin ⓭ Die ⓮ Pie ⓯ Compass

CHIMERA

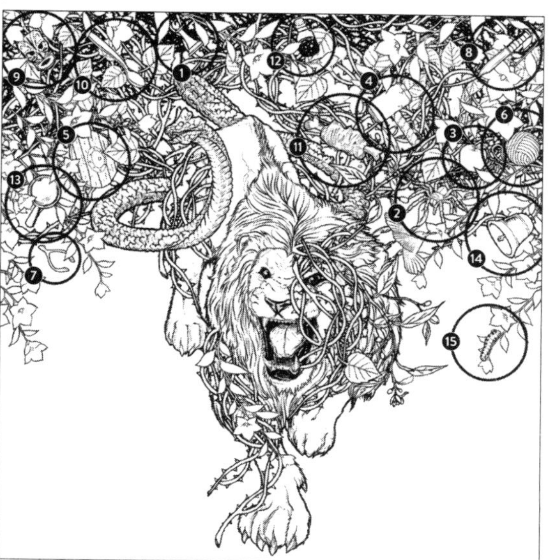

❶ Chess Piece - Bishop ❷ Spider ❸ Apple ❹ Hammer ❺ Wooden Shield ❻ Ball of Yarn ❼ Wishbone ❽ Knife ❾ Totem ❿ Spoon ⓫ Raw Meat and Bone ⓬ Potion Bottle ⓭ Magnifying Glass ⓮ Bell ⓯ Caterpillar

FRILLED-NECK LIZARD

❶ Cactus in a Pot ❷ Toothbrush ❸ Cookie ❹ Screw ❺ Shoe ❻ Button ❼ Matches ❽ Pan ❾ Spatula ❿ Thimble ⓫ Computer Mouse ⓬ Tape Measure ⓭ Rake ⓮ Coffee Mug ⓯ Alarm Clock

RABBIT

❶ Carrot ❷ Carton of Eggs ❸ Candy ❹ Watering Can ❺ Bow ❻ Paint Palette ❼ Headphones ❽ Frog ❾ Ice Cream Cone ❿ Safety Pin ⓫ Trumpet ⓬ Telescope ⓭ Bat ⓮ Spring ⓯ Boot

OWL

❶ Rune Stone ❷ Book ❸ Monocle ❹ Ink and Quill ❺ Witch Hat ❻ Present ❼ Wrench ❽ Yo-yo ❾ Cupcake ❿ Pipe ⓫ Rubber Stamp ⓬ Broom ⓭ Gold Bar ⓮ Rubik's Cube ⓯ Abacus

ELEPHANT

❶ Rune Stone ❷ Wind-up Mouse ❸ Bowling Pin ❹ Chess Piece - Pawn ❺ Pizza ❻ Bucket ❼ Baseball Bat ❽ Playing Card ❾ Safari Hat ❿ Drum ⓫ Peanut ⓬ Snake ⓭ Butterfly Net ⓮ Popcorn ⓯ Camera

CERBERUS

❶ Playing Card ❷ Rune Stone ❸ Chain ❹ Keys ❺ Gemstone ❻ Shovel ❼ Flashlight ❽ Pocket Knife ❾ Map ❿ Axe ⓫ Picture Frame ⓬ Crow ⓭ Puzzle Piece ⓮ Mousetrap ⓯ Fireworks

BUFFALO

❶ Woodpecker ❷ Pinwheel ❸ Burger ❹ Slice of Watermelon ❺ Pencil ❻ Toast ❼ Hand Bell ❽ Friendship Bracelet ❾ Origami - Airplane ❿ Corn ⓫ Whistle ⓬ Shuttlecock ⓭ Tongs ⓮ Popsicle ⓯ Bowtie

FENRIR (WOLF)

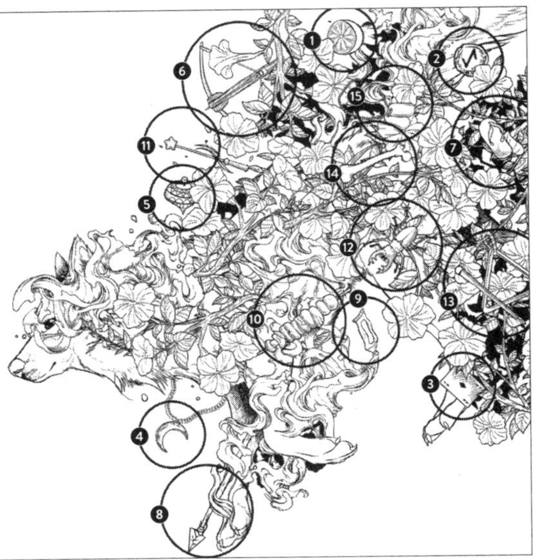

❶ Lemon ❷ Rune Stone ❸ Playing Card ❹ Moon Pendant ❺ Top ❻ Crossbow ❼ Flip-flops ❽ Spear ❾ Paint Tube ❿ Skewer ⓫ Wand ⓬ Stag Beetle ⓭ Music Triangle ⓮ Bone ⓯ Dog Tag

SEAHORSE

❶ Snorkel ❷ Flippers ❸ Propeller ❹ Starfish ❺ Jellyfish ❻ Bottle Cap ❼ Blowfish ❽ Soda Can ❾ Pearl Clam ❿ Turtle ⓫ Wristwatch ⓬ Ladle ⓭ Sponge ⓮ Soap ⓯ Seashell

KRAKEN

❶ Scuba Tank ❷ Paddle ❸ Anchor ❹ Surfboard ❺ Taco ❻ Life Preserver ❼ Goggles ❽ Treasure Chest ❾ Ship Wheel ❿ Hook ⓫ Message in a Bottle ⓬ Diver Helmet ⓭ Crab ⓮ Sea Urchin ⓯ Harpoon

TIGER

❶ Fan ❷ Samurai Sword ❸ Shuriken ❹ Wind Chime ❺ Medallion ❻ Kettle ❼ Paper Umbrella ❽ Wooden Sandals ❾ Origami - Crane ❿ Lantern ⓫ Gloves ⓬ Grasshopper ⓭ Rope ⓮ Straw Hat ⓯ Sushi Plate

TURTLE

❶ Sand Shovel and Bucket ❷ Doughnut ❸ Hermit Crab ❹ Shrimp ❺ Wooden Crate ❻ Eel ❼ Gramophone ❽ Wine Glass ❾ Playing Card ❿ Butter Knife ⓫ Coconut Drink ⓬ Pineapple ⓭ Frisbee ⓮ Movie Ticket ⓯ Cherries

WINGED LION

❶ Soccer Ball ❷ Shield ❸ Harmonica ❹ Rune Stone ❺ Goblet ❻ Grapes ❼ Rollerblades ❽ Bell Pepper ❾ Whip ❿ Gladiator Helmet ⓫ Golf Club ⓬ Earphones ⓭ Fang Necklace ⓮ Mail ⓯ Bowl of Soup

HIPPOCAMPUS

❶ Rune Stone ❷ Horseshoe ❸ Golf Ball ❹ Pretzel ❺ Wooden Barrel ❻ Unicycle ❼ Microphone ❽ Boxing Gloves ❾ Jump Rope ❿ Jackstone ⓫ Hotdog ⓬ Hockey Stick ⓭ Party Hat ⓮ Squid ⓯ Pearl Necklace

JELLYFISH

❶ Jewel ❷ Bottle Opener ❸ Jam and Bread ❹ Perfume ❺ Notepad ❻ Tiki Mask ❼ Gelatin Mold ❽ Fisherman's Hat ❾ Magnifying Glass ❿ Gold Coins ⓫ Thermometer ⓬ Stars ⓭ Moon ⓮ Sun ⓯ Fish

HAWK

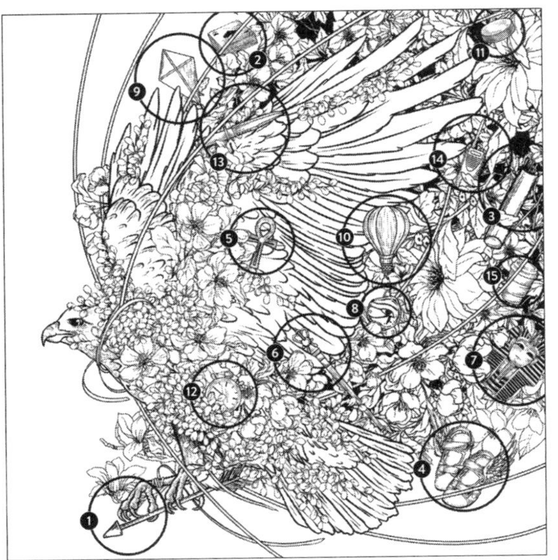

❶ Arrow ❷ Deck of Cards ❸ Quiver ❹ Winged Sandals ❺ Ankh ❻ Scepter ❼ Mummy Mask ❽ Eye of Horus ❾ Kite ❿ Hot Air Balloon ⓫ Hockey Puck ⓬ Stopwatch ⓭ Hunting Knife ⓮ Radio ⓯ Paper Cup

BEAR

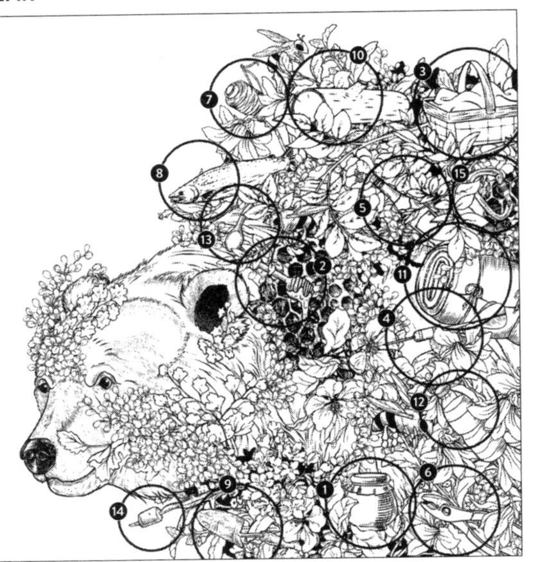

❶ Honey Pot ❷ Honey Stirrer ❸ Picnic Basket ❹ Dart ❺ Wine Bottle ❻ Pliers ❼ Thread ❽ Salmon ❾ Hand Trowel ❿ Log ⓫ Sleeping Bag ⓬ Water Bottle ⓭ Wooden Spoon ⓮ Marshmallow on a Stick ⓯ Carabiner

PHOENIX

❶ Viking Helmet ❷ Rune Stone ❸ Sun Pendant ❹ Justice Scale ❺ Emblem ❻ Earrings ❼ Fire Extinguisher ❽ Gas Mask ❾ Dumplings ❿ Barbecue ⓫ Fire Hydrant ⓬ Baguette ⓭ Barbecue Fork ⓮ Candle Holder ⓯ Lighter

LIONFISH

❶ Water Gun ❷ Can Opener ❸ Toy Shark ❹ Brass Knuckles ❺ Letter Opener ❻ Package ❼ Pencil Eraser ❽ Lantern Fish ❾ Sunken Boat ❿ Submarine ⓫ Chair ⓬ Straw and Cup ⓭ Totem ⓮ Shell Necklace ⓯ Lobster Trap

SNAIL

❶ Test Tubes ❷ Rune Stone ❸ Tag ❹ 3D Glasses ❺ Tweezers ❻ Dinosaur Skull ❼ Spider Web ❽ Cassette Tape ❾ Footprint ❿ Broccoli ⓫ Jellybeans ⓬ Spider ⓭ Garlic ⓮ Tomato ⓯ Ice Bucket

GRIFFIN

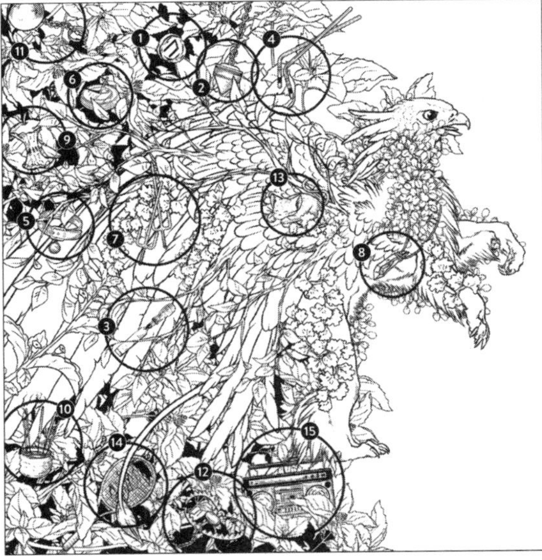

❶ Rune Stone ❷ Pendulum ❸ Chisel ❹ Dowsing Rod ❺ Dog Collar ❻ Sundial ❼ Sai ❽ Crystal Necklace ❾ Bitten Apple ❿ Incense ⓫ Ball and Chain ⓬ Bear Trap ⓭ Cat ⓮ Tennis Racket ⓯ Boombox

MONKEY

1 Banana 2 Telephone 3 Clown Wind-up Box 4 Bag of Chips 5 Pizza Cutter 6 Battery 7 Toilet Paper 8 Nunchucks 9 Iron 10 Graduation Cap 11 Skateboard 12 Moai Statue 13 Handcuffs 14 Slingshot 15 Table Tennis

HUMMINGBIRD

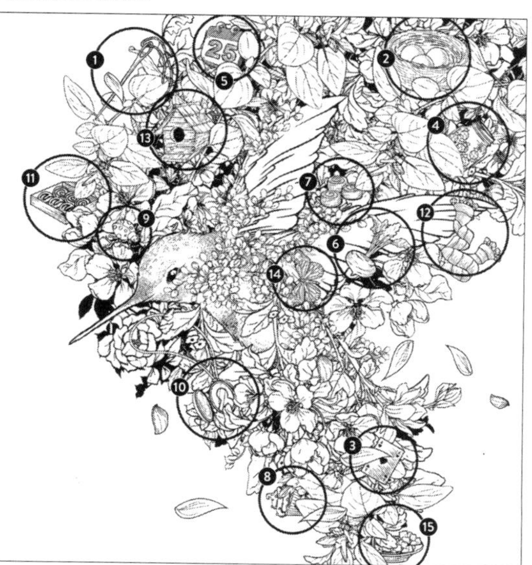

1 Needle 2 Bird's Nest 3 Playing Card 4 Jar of Candy 5 Calendar 6 Beet 7 Cinnamon Rolls 8 Cupcake 9 Ladybug 10 Locket 11 Box of Chocolates 12 Scarf 13 Birdhouse 14 Butterfly 15 Sugar Cubes

RAM

1 Shepherd's Staff 2 Shaving Knife 3 Toaster 4 Wooden Wheel 5 Wagon 6 Dove 7 Gavel 8 Hay 9 Pitchfork 10 Coffee Beans 11 Chili 12 Goat Bell 13 Potholder 14 Urn 15 Horn

WHALE

1 Fishing Pole 2 Seagull 3 Wood Plank 4 Boat 5 Stingray 6 Pirate Hat 7 Eye Patch 8 Pirate's Rum 9 Beach Ball 10 Scuba Diver 11 Coin Purse 12 Wooden Leg 13 Anchor 14 Treasure Map 15 Pirate Sword

CRAB

1 Slice of Pineapple 2 Rubber Band 3 Lug Wrench 4 Jewel 5 Rune Stone 6 Playing Card 7 Wind-up Chomping Teeth 8 Clown Nose 9 Eye Glasses 10 Coin Purse 11 Plant in a Jar 12 Slug 13 Protractor 14 Broken Pencil 15 Churros

STORK

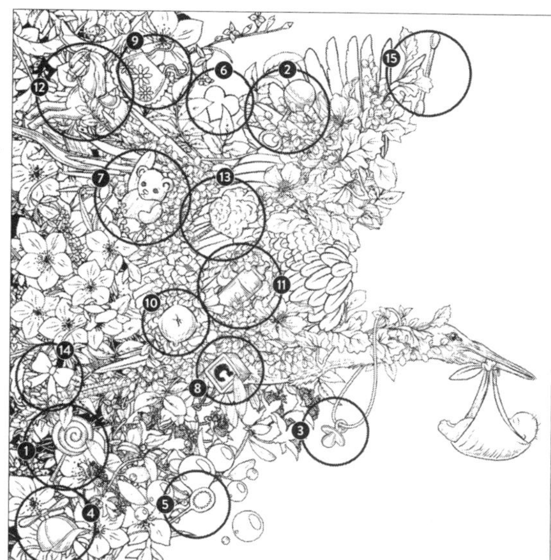

1 Lollipop 2 Baby Rattle 3 Pacifier 4 Propeller Hat 5 Bubble Toy 6 Heart 7 Teddy Bear 8 Letter Block 9 Baby Bib 10 Pillow 11 Baby Bottle 12 Rocking Horse 13 Cotton Candy 14 Bow 15 Cotton Buds

BAT

❶ Music Note ❷ Moon Key ❸ Blindfold ❹ Sonar Monitor ❺ Headphones ❻ Moth ❼ Chef's Hat ❽ Dart Board ❾ Gumball Machine ❿ Bingo Card ⓫ Scorpion ⓬ Bookworm ⓭ Spray Paint ⓮ Power Plug ⓯ Clipboard

HEDGEHOG

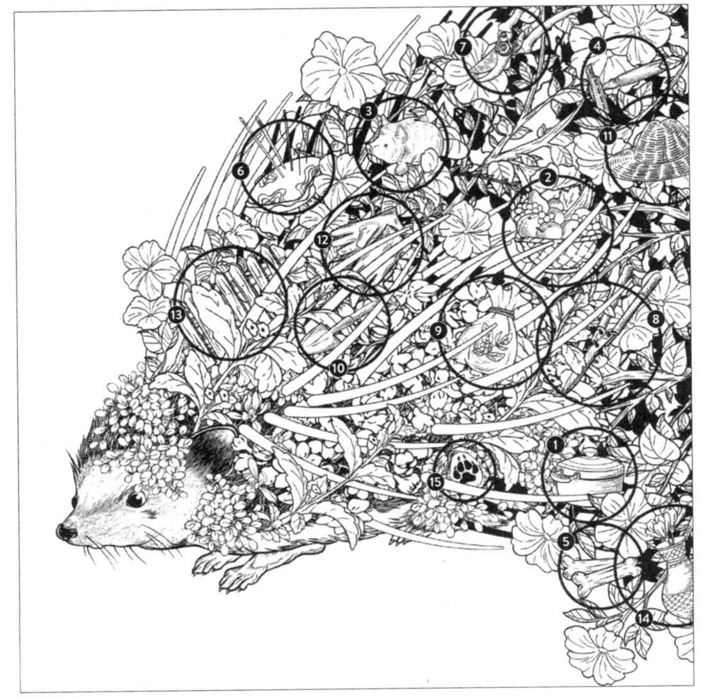

❶ Cooking Pot ❷ Basket of Fruit ❸ Piggy Bank ❹ Razor ❺ Dog Bones ❻ Pin Cushion ❼ Hedge Shears ❽ Pruning Shears ❾ Fertilizer ❿ Trowel ⓫ Straw Hat ⓬ Gardening Gloves ⓭ Picket Fence ⓮ Flower in a Vase ⓯ Paw Print

FROG

❶ Garden Gnome ❷ Top Hat ❸ Magician's Wand ❹ Sun Key ❺ Cane ❻ Sock ❼ Fly ❽ Wooden Sign ❾ Spotlight ❿ Trophy ⓫ World Globe ⓬ Diamond ⓭ Clothes Hanger ⓮ Koi ⓯ Handkerchief

CHEETAH

❶ Sausage ❷ Fried Egg ❸ Bolt of Lightning ❹ Rune Stone ❺ Running Shoes ❻ Toy Train ❼ Speedometer ❽ Jewel ❾ Checkered Flag ❿ Sun Visor ⓫ Cricket Bat ⓬ Lizard ⓭ Bicycle Helmet ⓮ Traffic Cone ⓯ Vinyl Record

CHAMELEON

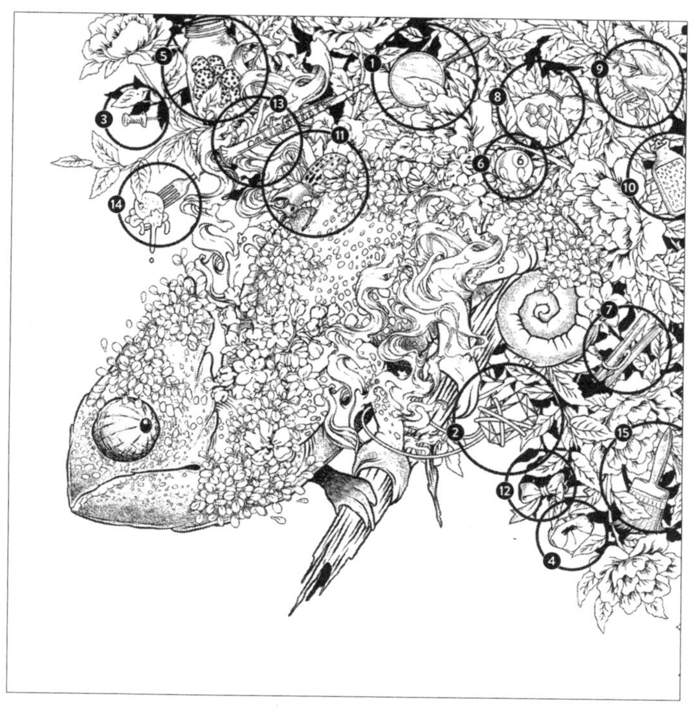

❶ Mirror ❷ Jewel ❸ Thumbtack ❹ Amber ❺ Jar of Cookies ❻ Billiard Ball ❼ Clothespins ❽ Bag of Marshmallows ❾ Fortune Cookie ❿ Hot Compress ⓫ Beetle ⓬ Bow ⓭ Clarinet ⓮ Fork and Meatball ⓯ Paint Brush

STINGRAY

❶ Tap ❷ Float Tube ❸ Crab Claw ❹ Nautilus ❺ Fish Bone ❻ Ice Pick ❼ Volleyball ❽ Baby Octopus ❾ Oil Barrel ❿ Swordfish ⓫ Tiki ⓬ Pearl Ring ⓭ Origami - Fish ⓮ Rope ⓯ Sunglasses

SNAKE

❶ Dice ❷ Crystal ❸ Poison Bottle ❹ Mouse ❺ Safety Goggles ❻ Laboratory Flask ❼ Scalpel ❽ Doctor's Mask ❾ Recorder ❿ First Aid Kit ⓫ Ice Pack ⓬ Flashlight ⓭ Cracked Egg ⓮ Ginger Root ⓯ Clay Pot

CARABAO

❶ Mango ❷ Crowbar ❸ Wind Turbine ❹ Sickle ❺ Paint Can ❻ Paper Bag ❼ Toolbox ❽ Miner's Pick ❾ Sombrero ❿ Potato Sack ⓫ Sprout ⓬ Plow ⓭ Wheelbarrow ⓮ Chicken

SWAN

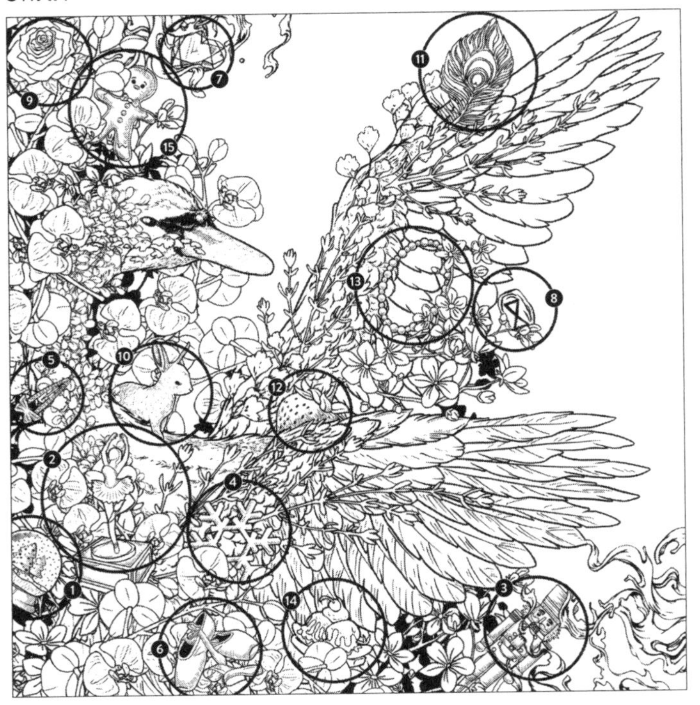

1 Snow Globe 2 Music Box 3 Nutcracker 4 Snowflake 5 Hair Pin 6 Ballet Shoes 7 Heart Jewel 8 Rune Stone 9 Rose 10 Bunny 11 Peacock Feather 12 Strawberry 13 Pearl Bracelet 14 Ice Cream Sundae 15 Gingerbread Man

FOX

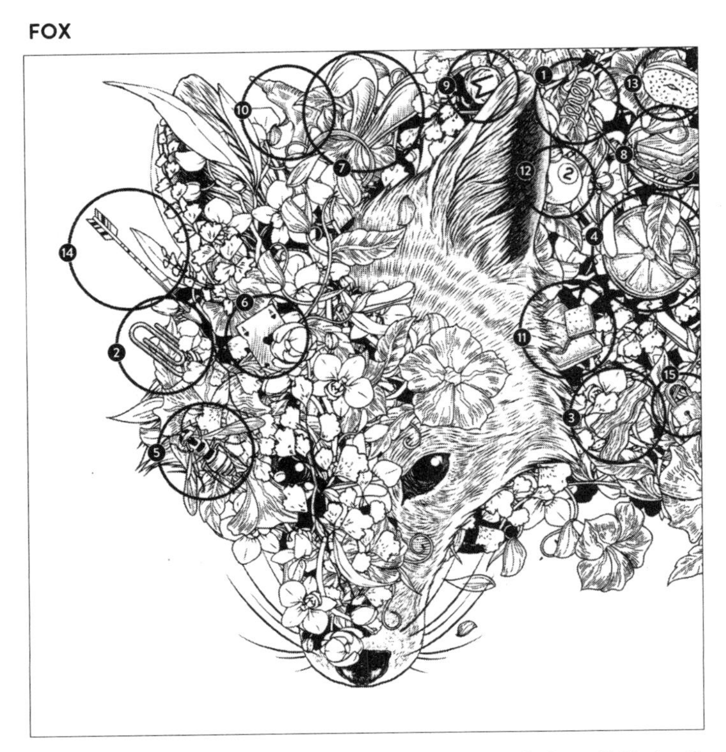

1 Corndog 2 Paper Clip 3 Bacon 4 Slice of Orange 5 Wasp 6 Playing Card 7 Rabbit-Ears Headband 8 Sandwich 9 Rune Stone 10 Glue Gun 11 Biscuit 12 Billiard Ball 13 Bagel 14 Arrow 15 Lock

EEL

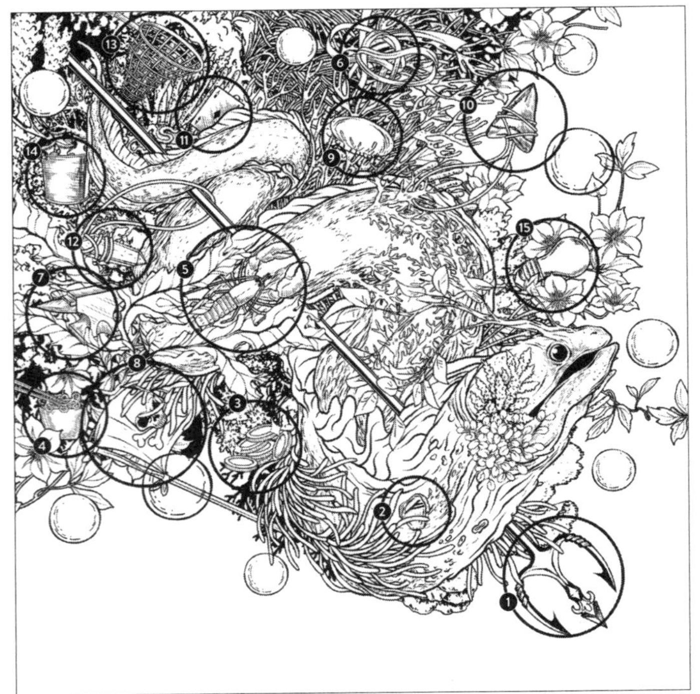

1 Trident 2 Rune Stone 3 Gold Coins 4 Noodles 5 Lobster 6 Ribbon Lasso 7 Anvil 8 Pirate Flag 9 Shower Cap 10 Shark Tooth Necklace 11 Playing Card 12 Crystal Necklace 13 Fishing Net 14 Fish Bucket 15 Lightbulb

MOOSE

1 Strawberry 2 Rune Stone 3 Knitting Needles and Yarn 4 Stocking 5 Mushrooms 6 Megaphone 7 Teapot 8 Totem 9 Clapperboard 10 Typewriter 11 Native American Headdress 12 Lasso 13 Squirrel 14 Jewel 15 Caterpillar

CAPRICORN

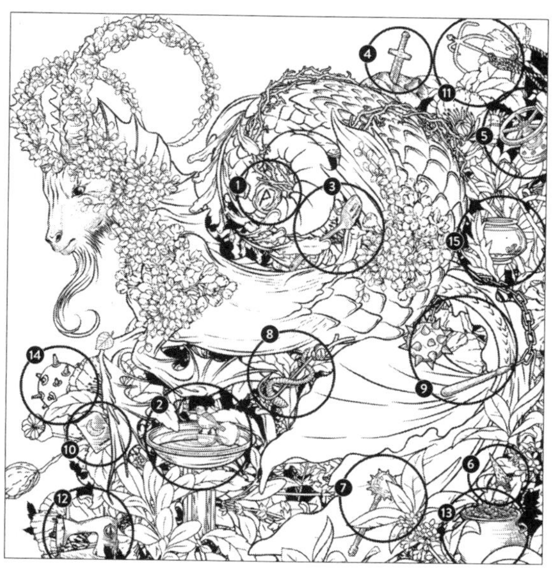

❶ Rune Stone ❷ Bird Bath ❸ Slotted Spoon ❹ Sword in a Stone ❺ Valve ❻ Arrowhead ❼ Flail ❽ Fishing Lure ❾ Mace ❿ Tarot Card ⓫ Grappling Hook ⓬ Sewing Machine ⓭ Pot of Gold ⓮ Naval Mine ⓯ Fishbowl

CAT

❶ Ball of Yarn ❷ Milk Carton ❸ Jingle Bell ❹ Mouse ❺ Crystal Ball ❻ Lucky Cat ❼ Pumpkin ❽ Four-leaf Clover ❾ Rune Stone ❿ Tea Bag ⓫ Funnel ⓬ Whisk ⓭ Adhesive Bandage ⓮ Butter ⓯ Feather

PEGASUS

❶ Rune Stone ❷ Caduceus ❸ Billiard Ball ❹ Saddle ❺ Jewel ❻ Circlet ❼ Hummingbird ❽ Winged Helmet ❾ Playing Card ❿ Macaroons ⓫ Toy Airplane ⓬ Hammer ⓭ Belt ⓮ Goblet ⓯ Cowboy Hat

DRAGON

❶ Sword ❷ Helm ❸ Shield ❹ Torch ❺ Playing Card ❻ Gauntlet ❼ Crown ❽ Rune Stone ❾ Spinning Wheel ❿ Satchel ⓫ Cannon ⓬ Puppet ⓭ Firecracker ⓮ Sheriff Badge ⓯ Cauldron

WALRUS

❶ Heart Ring ❷ Penguin ❸ Ice Cubes ❹ Sled ❺ Ice Skate ❻ Candy Cane ❼ Icicles ❽ Santa Hat ❾ Playing Card ❿ Snowman ⓫ Jewel ⓬ Spoon ⓭ Aviator Hat ⓮ Goggles ⓯ Cherries

TARSIER

❶ Peeler ❷ Avocado ❸ Banana Peel ❹ Jingle Bells ❺ Bag of Marbles ❻ Doorknob ❼ Parrot ❽ Xylophone ❾ Poker Chip ❿ Bone ⓫ TV Remote ⓬ Kettlebell ⓭ Cucumber ⓮ Spool ⓯ Snail

RACCOON

❶ Calculator ❷ Bag of Beans ❸ Pinecone ❹ Stapler ❺ Cheese ❻ Ice Cream Scooper ❼ Salt Shaker ❽ Slice of Cake ❾ Pepper Grinder ❿ Trash Can ⓫ Panda ⓬ Rune Stone ⓭ Sack ⓮ Medicine Dropper ⓯ Ramen

GIRAFFE

❶ Necktie ❷ Postage Stamp ❸ Pencil Sharpener ❹ Corkscrew ❺ Rune Stone ❻ Billiard Ball ❼ Jewel ❽ Butterfly ❾ Bread ❿ Spell Book ⓫ Suitcase ⓬ Beehive ⓭ Artichoke ⓮ Sunflower ⓯ Ladder

PEACOCK

❶ Scarf ❷ Rune Stone ❸ Pickle ❹ Bread ❺ Fedora ❻ Diamond Necklace ❼ Party Blower ❽ Star Key ❾ Oil Bottle ❿ Rattle Drum Toy ⓫ Theatre Faces ⓬ Feather Duster ⓭ Chopped Wood

ZEBRA

❶ Zipper ❷ Jewel ❸ Nesting Dolls ❹ Playing Card ❺ Squeegee ❻ Rune Stone ❼ Domino ❽ Arrow in Apple ❾ Wallet ❿ Bow ⓫ Scroll ⓬ Billiard Ball ⓭ Pen ⓮ Succulents in a Jar ⓯ Leprechaun Hat

OTTER

❶ Croissant ❷ Grater ❸ Rune Stone ❹ Peanut Butter ❺ Periscope ❻ Jewel ❼ Thermos ❽ Hatchet ❾ Bowl of Rice ❿ Baked Potato ⓫ Clam ⓬ Cooler ⓭ Steak ⓮ Papaya ⓯ Basket

GAZELLE

❶ Balloon Animal ❷ Billiard Ball ❸ Stethoscope ❹ Jewel ❺ Fries ❻ Rune Stone ❼ Playing Card ❽ Newspaper ❾ Chalk Box ❿ Cork ⓫ Bag of Money ⓬ Bird ⓭ Slice of Lemon ⓮ Unicorn Horn ⓯ Dustpan

BUTTERFLY

❶ Brooch ❷ Blimp ❸ Accordion ❹ Crystal ❺ Strawberry Jam ❻ Nightcap ❼ Lychee ❽ Jewel ❾ Waffle ❿ Flower in Glass Case ⓫ Tiara ⓬ Hair Comb ⓭ Earmuffs ⓮ Letter Blocks ⓯ Balloon

GORILLA

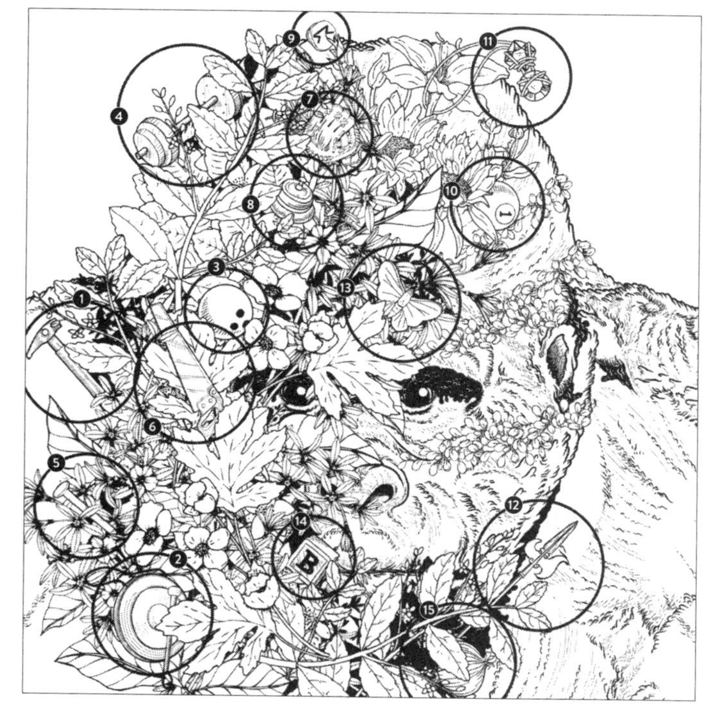

❶ Climbing Pick ❷ Gong ❸ Bowling Ball ❹ Dumbbell ❺ Nail ❻ Hand Saw ❼ Baseball Glove ❽ Service Bell ❾ Rune Stone ❿ Billiard Ball ⓫ Jewel ⓬ Halberd ⓭ Moth ⓮ Letter Block ⓯ Onion

MYTHOGRAPHIC COLOR AND DISCOVER: ANIMALS.

For information, address St. Martin's Press, 175 Fifth Avenue, New York, N.Y. 10010.

www.stmartins.com

www.castlepointbooks.com

The Castle Point Books trademark is owned by Castle Point Publishing, LLC.

Castle Point books are published and distributed by St. Martin's Press.

ISBN 978-1-250-19985-0 (trade paperback)

Cover Design by Young Lim

Edited by Monica Sweeney

Our books may be purchased in bulk for promotional, educational, or business use. Please contact your local bookseller or the Macmillan Corporate and Premium Sales Department at 1-800-221-7945, extension 5442, or by email at MacmillanSpecialMarkets@macmillan.com.

First Edition: September 2018

10 9 8 7 6 5 4 3 2 1